# In Praise of
## *Red Memory*

With a sure poetic touch, Amy Bobeda takes us through a tangled dreamscape of red threads converging in a liberating new understanding of the world's most ancient taboo.

—**Chris Knight**, *Blood Relations.*

*Red Memory* is a vibrant tour of menstrual myth, poetry and ritual experience.

—**Camilla Power**

Amy Bobeda's *Red Memory* is a perfect book in so many ways. First of all, I learned a lot from it. Then there's the fact that it rescues Charles Olson's concept of the saturation job—for the good of the matriarchy! Finally it leaves the reader with the lovely sensation of swimming into "the red thread of humanity's continued birth" (yes, menstrual blood). I appreciate the opportunity to open that old wound, shepherded along by a fine young poet.

—**Lisa Jarnot**, *Robert Duncan,*
*The Ambassador from Venus: A Biography*

*Red Memory* is a stunning multi-layered poem of what we need to know of telluric menses power. Amy Bobeda's generative book is rich with investigation, meditation, nocturnal thrum, cyclical ritual, complexity of blood-flow, that includes vivid dreams, synchronous sympathetic animalia, cave-lore, paint and psychic adornment. It is also a potent performance with an extended river of language, evocative collages and tension on its pages. Here we attune and attend to blood as glorious menses, as lyric sister, as what makes the world turn, as in the striking detail of the shiny red lycra suits the backup singers wear with JLo and Shakira at half time.

I was struck by the poet's astute observation of how we bleed the world around us projecting blood letting on the outer sphere with fracking, oil drilling and horrors of war, and simultaneously eschew the inner world of healing, gnosis and celebration. *Red Memory* is an untethered, passionate and bold mini-epic feeling as primordial as blood itself.

—**Anne Waldman**, *Trickster Feminism*

# Red Memory

FLOWERSONG
PRESS

by
**Amy Bobeda**

**FLOWERSONG**
P R E S S

FlowerSong Press
Copyright © 2022 by Amy Bobeda
ISBN: 978-1-953447-36-4
Library of Congress Control Number: 2022950136

Published by FlowerSong Press
in the United States of America.
www.flowersongpress.com

Cover Photo by amu on Unsplash.com
Cover Design by Priscilla Celina Suarez
Set in Adobe Garamond Pro

NOTICE: SCHOOLS AND BUSINESSES

FlowerSong Press offers copies of this book at quantity discount with bulk
purchase for educational, business, or sales promotional use. For information,
please email the Publisher at info@flowersongpress.com.

For menstruants, past, present, and future.

# TABLE OF CONTENTS

*Image: Wonderland*......2
Introduction......3

*Day 1*......9
*la nube*......10
*hechizo seco*......11
*pursuit of.*......12
*Image: Grief*......13
untitled......14
*rainbow genesis*......15
untitled......16
*how we became different*......17
*a loop being forms*......18
*Image: clots*......19
*the symphony of flutes*......20
*writing came later*......21
*Image: Pillow*......22
*Day 734*......23
*Mound Mound*......24
*Day earth was created*......28

*Sexual birth......*29

*Pleiades......*30

*Image: Spotting......*31

*Alchemy of Dreams......*32

*The blood skirt......*33

*Image: Ear......*33

*Skirt Bleeds......*34

*Embroidering a blood skirt......*35

*Image: Venus cries over rags......*37

*Rags......*38

*Image: Red Hot Blood......*40

*Image: In the Grass......*42

*Day 2......*44

*Ovulatory dream, day 13......*45

*Musgos......*47

*Image: Seclusion......*48

*Fox Woman Dreaming......*49

*Aliento, Day 12......*52

*The machine embroiders......*54

*Prayers for menstruation......*55

*Empathy......*56

*Day 16......*57

*Image: The gift......*58

*The merge......*59

*Day 3 first snow......*60

*Unnamed Dream......*61

*In time......*62

*Image: Marked......*63

*Day 11 ......*64

*Day 4......*65

*Ochre......*66

*medicina de los sueños......*67

*Image: blood sweets......*68

*depression in dreams bleeds......69*
*day twenty-nine and ½......70*
*an ear dreaming......71*
*Image: Medicine......72*
*on lamenting silence......73*
*day 15......75*
*Image: Bare down......76*
*Image: Belly......77*
*Lonely days fullness......78*
*Day 8......79*
*Image: The Belly II......80*
*Mating season......81*
*confusing our blood with blood......82*
*Image: a spatter......83*
*Image: Synchrony......84*
*Day 22......85*
*ambas y nada......86*
*rites of passage......87*
*day 34......88*
*cuerpo......89*
*Image: untitled woman.....90*
*day 27......91*
*Waiting......92*
*remembrance for a loss of sound......93*

People of note......97
Reading List......99
Acknowledgements......101
About the Author......103

# Red Memory

A prairie dog salutes the sun.

A red tail body checks bald eagle.

Something about this time feels like starting over. Like when the moon

reaches day 29.5.

Like the day I discovered Marija Gimbutas decoded a language on goddess figurines. Most anthropologists and archeologists did not believe her. But she rose before dawn each morning to write on an Apple 2E about the secret language of the goddess. Each line and curve made blood, milk, honey, water: gifts of earth mother.

∿∿∿

The anthropologists I know say "I wonder why Venus figurines did not have feet." My mother, who builds figurative porcelain sculptures, would say "Feet are hard." When laboring over carving mammoth tusk and bone, who bothers with feet? Feet are not food. I see the tip of each Venus' single leg stuck firmly into the ground, earth becoming toes becoming stylus. A tiny woman carved in bone enveloped by soil writing herself into being.

∿∿∿

It is said the prairie dog is more linguistically developed than other non-human mammals. I live surrounded by these curious creatures who delicately groom each other's faces, rise to greet predators, and chirp into the wind each morning. I begin to wonder if the origin of their language connects to their reproductive cycles—primates, bats, elephant shrew, and spiny mouse are the only mammals besides humans who shed uterine lining.

∿∿∿

"The business of stories is not enchantment. The business of stories is waking up."
—Martin Shaw

∿∿∿

In the tale of The Wawilak Sisters, two sisters in Arnhem Land, Australia, travel from their homeland. The older sister carries her young son strapped to her body; the younger is quite pregnant from incestuous sex with a clansman. Like many cultures, incest is a great taboo in Aboriginal mythology—kin extend beyond human families.

The sisters carry spears, very uncharacteristic behavior for Wawilak women, not because women cannot hunt, but rather because they do not have to. But the Wawilak Sisters are on their own with no intention of returning home; they hunt small game and gather plants for dinner along their journey. They give each animal and plant its first name.

Soon, the women grow tired and set up camp near a watering hole with a small hut and fire. They toss a wombat on the fire who springs to life and runs away. The next dances into the night. Every animal they name and kill revives in the fire, fleeing into the Australian wilderness.

By the fire, the older sister begins to menstruate, her blood flowing into the watering hole, home of the infamous Rainbow Snake. It is well known that the Rainbow Snake, bringer of floods, thunder, and rain, both loves and hates the sacred profane sight and smell of menstrual blood. As blood swirls into water, the snake grows angry and the weather begins to change. A large storm cloud appears, conjured from blue sky. Rain pours.

The second sister goes into labor. Together the women deliver a healthy baby boy as the red post-birth fluid of the new mother mixes with her sister's menstrual blood, seeping into the pool. In some versions of the story, the women sit, legs splayed open, and loop threads of blood over their hands and arms, creating the world's first cat's cradle, still played by women today.

The post-birth blood is too much for the Rainbow Snake to bear; the storm worsens and the women retreat into the hut where they dance and sing through the night to keep the Snake at bay. More blood flows into the watering hole and the storm worsens. Eventually, so agitated and aroused, the Rainbow Snake gets rid of them by swallowing the women and children whole. The Snake rears up into the sky as the flood water rises to meet it, consuming the land in water. Meanwhile, the women and children, still very much alive in its belly, make the Snake's stomach grumble. The Snake spits them out, only to swallow them once more. Snakes from each clan across the land raise their heads into the sky to join the Rainbow Snake, who regurgitates the Wawilak Sisters one last time.

As it spits the sisters and their children into the sky the Snake hisses out the first dialects for each clan across the continent. The Wawilak Sisters and their sons turn to stone, still seen today on journeys across what is now Australia.

When the Snake finally calms, flood waters recede as two men pass by the watering hole. "Wrong-way Snake," they say, "what have you done? Those sisters were not just any sisters, they were your kin." The Snake in turn gives the men the sacred dance of the Wawilak Sisters, which is still passed down today.

~~~

Mythologist Martin Shaw writes, "Words can constrict, words can liberate," just as the snake and women dance in the cosmic cycle of death and rebirth. "Things happen when you start to speak…thinking in myth teaches us how to speak." A word, like menstrual blood, is both sacred and profane, ebbing and flowing in relationship with other words. This mysterious and nebulous relationality of language rests heavily in menstrual taboos. Like the understanding bleeding into the pool will anger the Rainbow Snake and bring storms, the opposite is also true: not giving menstrual blood to earth and water may result in drought. Language mimics the menstrual paradox as words say one thing and another simultaneously; we lose meaning in our perception of words and phrases not in language itself.

~~~

Literal menstruation is the secret work of menstruants: the red thread of humanity's continued birth. Metaphorical and symbolic menstruation is legible, yet barred from social conversation. This dichotomy is part of blood's ritual potency which leads cultures around the world to usurp the power of blood through ceremonies of male menstruation. In this power-switching menstruation disappears from discourse. The natural flow becomes forced and controlled; men cut noses, ankles, and penises to mimic menses. Tampons become scented. Women world-wide drop out of school to tend their cycles or take contraception to make them disappear.

~~~

In accounts of human origins, social anthropologist, Chris Knight says human culture's first metaphor was likening a bleeding woman to the blood of the sacred animal. In Africa, the eland bull, in Australia, the kangaroo. This metaphor made women's blood the sacred symbol of death and rebirth. Menstruation, post-birth, and miscarriage blood transformed the woman into the animal sacrificed to feed our ancestors. Once cooked, the kangaroo nourished and sustained human life, allowing women to bleed, become pregnant, and bleed again in childbirth. To keep balance and cyclicity of blood, A man could not touch a bleeding woman nor could he eat the raw meat of his own kill. In this world, women secluded together during menstruation, their sequester dictated by the moon.

Knight theorizes women developed female coalitions to protect menstruats from rape. Despite our modern associations with menstruation, biologically the menstruant allures. She is, in a sense, sexy: her blood a sign of imminent fertility. In the practice of female solidarity, women gathered and painted their bodies red with blood, ochre, and fat to collectively signal that they were the bleeding kangaroo and could not be eaten. Their bleeding bodies became the first word for 'no'. Their solidarity echoes in today's Avon parties and MAC's universally flattering and popular *ruby woo* lipstick.

In more recent work, Knight theorizes language emerged from the sound of laughter. The language tethered between humor and sounds of opposition.

～～～

In *The Read Thread, The Story of the Red Thread,* Cecilia Vicuña traces this origin of female solidarity through the cat's cradle and the red thread as an umbilical cord from mother to child, woman to woman, to earth. In one poem she writes:

| the open letters | are hand/legs | sustaining the strands of history | the future of the world held | by women's culture of solidarity | of women's menstruation | blood pours down the page

Through the myth of the Wawilak Sisters she likens letters to the body, letters forming out of the cat's cradle of menstrual and post-birth threads, and the thread of forgotten history: language is menstrual.

～～～

The poet Penelope Shuttle writes in her book *Alchemy for Women*, "Women are the greatest dreamers," and "the menstrual cycle is the dream cycle." Suggesting sleep transports dreamers to the liminal world of myth conjured by the Rainbow Snake where we are born and resurrected each night we fall asleep. "A word is pregnant with other words," Vicuña writes in another poem, always gestating, recycling, birthing from itself like an endless stream of dreams.

∿∿∿

I'm unsure how Marija Gimbutas convinced herself she could reveal the forgotten secret language of the Goddess. I stared at the computer for months wondering why it was so hard to say *menstruation is the origin of language*.

I began to braid a rug from the plastic bags that accumulated despite my best intentions. Threading pink and red fabrics to lectures on human origins, I braided plastic into thread, weaving myself back in time. I built an endless snake coiled upon itself.

I embroidered the Rainbow Snake on an old shirt. Weaving a red sun, raining over the few stains I never bothered to remove. I gave the snake several layers of skin; it grew, and I began to understand the simplicity of writing.

> "Awakening to itself, the thread remembers birthing."
> —Cecilia Vicuña

*The female rain, like the female initiate, is visualized as red.*
– Ian Watts citing Camilla Power

*Day One*

A wing. A beak. A breast. A break in silence that resonates a single tone.
*Sheeeeeeeewooooooooooooooh*

Assonance of wordless language. The uptick in clotting.  Body bears down as
witness to God.  Home becomes empty house in mourning.  Another
                                        feather dismantles     temor
                        de separación.



The eagle is a lover. The demon lover a ploy. The crow tempts the eagle. The
red tail body checks the space between whiteness.

El binaro imaginado.


                                                Imaginary
                                blue.

*la nube*

Rain came *red* on all their houses a snake

in grass building passage

carnelian          rosewood          cinnabar          ochre

carmine

       tuscan    russet              land flooded

auburn

crops died

as sun rose for worship

still

red

moon died and

men

struck flint across their noses

over ground

currant

longing for water.

Periodic rhythm could slow down and halt the flow of events, *or* it could accelerate and plunge the world into chaos.

It is equally conceivable that women might cease to menstruate and bear children, *or* that they might bleed continuously and give birth haphazardly. In either case, the sun and the moon, the heavenly bodies governing the alternation of day and night and of the seasons, would no longer be able to perform their function.

–Lévi-Strauss

*hechizo seco*

we steal time from the body

for fear
women will bleed endless
streams

wilting wheat
witches of the sun and moon
destroying progress

for fear
red rain
will never dry

a withered sun
predicting
end times

a harvest moon of
women's secrets.

Traditional tribal lifestyles are more often gynocratic than
not, and they are never patriarchal. These features make
understanding tribal cultures essential to all responsible activists
who seek life-affirming social change that can result in a real
decrease in human and planetary destruction and in a real
increase in quality of life for all inhabitants of planet earth.

—Paula Gunn Allen

The menstruant's gaze possessed a special ability to inflict harm --- the Evil Eye. The Evil Eye
can cause crops to fail, food to rot, babies to fall sick. Amulets, arm bands, and all manner of
charms are still worn in many regions of rural Europe, the Middle East, and North Africa, to
guard against it. According to ancient texts, there was also an "Eye of Life," the bestowing of
which was a blessing, recalled in such phrases as "look kindly upon" or "beneficent gaze." The
Evil Eye has gotten much more attention, however, especially since it was believed to be as
much involuntary as voluntary, making its power that much more in need of control.

—Judy Grahn

*pursuit of*
*PHILOSPHER'S STONE*

turning lead into gold

               both chemistry
               and metaphor   cooking       melting
reducing self to
               essence only to begin again

               most alchemical manuscripts feature bodies and
birds in glass vessels:
               crystal wombs
               dream lead into gold each sleep turning
         black   white   red

               green a complementary color

gadflies granted menses——
there were no words before *estrus.*

*menstrua* once *solūtiō*
dissolves
red pebbles in water

women                    sticky   leave the forest
*red* a hand painted stone

annotates our imperfections


la lengua symbol's memory
——————————————————————————pink permeates——

the shower a study of blood

dreamed by a single dreamer *we*

labor *red* into language

*rainbow genesis*

seven balls of thread braid
the rainbow

a girl eyes a white gash across
the sky swooping
the red parrot twirls, pricks
between her legs

————————————stringing—————————

to the rainbow
a man falls down dead

like
leaf divining bowl the
girl bleeds
red congealing jello.

hvísla
on wind water's teeth
hwistlōną
she is a snake in blood        so sing we
whistling

*what does a whistle look like in verbs?*

*sheeeeeeeeeeeeeewaaaaaaaaaaa*      *heeeeeeeeeeeeeewaaaaaaaaaaahhhh*

*ooooooooooooooooooo* oooooooooooooooooooooooooooo   *ooo* oooooooooo   oooooooooo  oo o     o

           words
           between
           words     bleed
     seed           breed
                    original language

A word is in first place a noise.
—Ursula K. Le Guin

16

*how we became different*

forest ears warble

polyphonic spirits
           blue from blame
           sprout

           pants sanguine now tired
           st. Margaret of Antioch

           discolored in modernity
springs from

blue dragon's belly into

               anger's lagoon
               she dives head first as
               red shines

on dark moon    our cycle (silence) begins–

The forest is the dream of animals and plants, the dream where we belong, yet we are destroying it fast.

                                      —Cecilia Vicuña

*a loop being forms*

∾

      sometimes dead prairie dogs smile     in relief
                and digress into another variant of
Paleolithic DNA.

      Our sisters'     sisters'       sisters'           mother
was a black bodied woman in Africa
so was ours

we called her *African Eve*

∞

before we named our colors
there were three—darkness, lightness, *red*.

Our babies built from termite dust; *perception* became genetic disorder.

∞

Moving from the known towards the unknown, symbolic culture was well established across Africa by 130 kya. I have argued that regular and ubiquitous use of red ochre provides a proxy for habitual collective ritual, transcending here-and-now contexts, with ritual performers across vast landscapes participating in shared fictions.

—Ian Watts

These are the only colors for which Ndembu possess primary terms. Terms for other colors are either derivates from these—as in the case of *chitookolo,* "gray", which is derived from *tooka,* "white"—or consist of descriptive and metaphorical phrases, as in the case of "green," *meji amatamba,* which means "water of sweet potato leaves." Very frequently, colors that we would distinguish from white, red and black are by Ndembu linguistically identified *with* them.

—Victor Turner

*the symphony of flutes*

Prometheus steals fire
humans steal voice from wind
man steals ritual potency from woman.

Women keep sacred flutes; one day men trick them away from music. One
day men steal their dilly bags. Run quartz across their ankles. Once men
bleed, women have nothing
or so it seems.

\*

"When painted, women inspired terror as they impersonated 'the spirits'.
They organized in a fearsome 'hut', but men eventually stormed this, taking
it over and performing in it exactly the same rituals as the women had done
before."—Chris Knight

\*

The dilly bag a fanny pack external uterus mistaken birth canal vagina the
dilly bag woven from *dili* fibers hair plant matter on strings for women
collecting food. The source of sustenance power pouch of a Kangaroo
mother.

A girl's first sewing project, a pillow case or dilly bag a pillow case on string
may develop into a cosmetics bag when she develops the skill of zippers
develops the dexterity to turn corners without sewing her thumb.

\*

In a rare version of *Jack and the Beanstalk*: once Jack reaches first creation
land of Sky the giant cuts the tip of his nose. Bleeding profusely, Jack
becomes the menarchal girl in a topsy turvy world, the signal of man
controlling man controlling nature culture ogres.

The world we live in is inherently upside down. Carnival lasts the cycle of the sun the cycle of the sun creates time devoid of matter. In 1474 a rooster was burned at the stake for witchcraft after laying an egg the lair of the cockatrice serpent with a rooster's head.

\*

The bullroarer is the sacred flute the *whuuuuuuuuuuuo whuuuuuuuuuuuuo whuuuuuuuuuuuuo whuuuuuuuuuuuuo* thrum the air a heartbeat return to womb.

> Women are told,
> "stay inside it's a female-devouring monster."

*whuuuuuuuuuuuuo whuuuuuuuuuuuuo whuuuuuuuuuuuuo whuuuuuuuuuuuuo*

Two women intended from a dream a magical flute which plays itself until men took the flutes and blew on them until women got so upset, they said,

> "go ahead, keep them."

A woman kept the flute under her skirt until one day her brother reached under her hem and snatched it. When he blew on the flute his sister's pubic hair jumped onto his face. The sound caused first menstruation: the origin of facial hair.

Kouroumbingac first woman invented everything gave birth alone misused her power killing too many animals so man took her sacred flute away and gave birth to boys without the help of women.

"Flutes needed feeding with meat. One day, the men – who were the hunters – threatened to withhold what they caught unless the women surrendered the flutes. Frightened of angering the fertility-spirits contained in the flutes, the women agreed, and the men seized the flutes and the power, which they have held to this day. (Murphy 1973: 217–18)"

—Chris Knight

In 2019, a man in Wisconsin tried to steal a flute by putting it down his pants. "I couldn't in good conscience let anyone ever put their lips to that instrument," said the store owner who turned the flute into a lamp.


on the rock

                eagle pecks                mouth  wound  vulva

Prometheus dies

              blood of Christ

                          male menarchal rite


        in me there is a sacrifice


                      underworld      deeper life's

communal resurrection

*writing came later*

inviting form outside the body
                              word

              ochres breasts and bellies
                                        attuned to scent

                        of nature not letter
                                   but rather blood
                                               life

                         *thrum*

           *thrum*
                                   *thrum*

                                   *thrum*

language sewing bodies  human

                              animal

                              word

*Day 734*

Many days I did not bleed  and the woman asked

"If you are not pregnant, why do you care."

    All the while     iron

                                      pebbles dip between
                       medicine and poison—

last to go
hemorrhaging
ochre three geese under the braided towel

*shheee*       *sheee*     *sheee*    *sssh*       *shhh*  *shh*    *sh sssssssssssss*

                         "why don't you?"

After six months without menstruating, my menses finally came back April first, so I painted my menstruation. No one ever paints menstruation, or shitting because they are idiots.  Can there be anything more beautiful than those red threads of blood? Clots of blood of surprising colors and shapes? Like abstracting paintings, Dekoonings and Pollocks coming out of the vagina? To see them is fascinating and not speak of them, hiding them is a forbidden act. To live in secret.

—Cecilia Vicuña

*Mound Mound*

A man from Albuquerque asks, "Did they really sleep down here?"

"No," the docent responds with a small grin, "there are no records, of course, but it's believed early man took to the caves for spiritual experience." We look to the stalactites and mites, millennia of water moving bits of sand, and see it hanging in the cool air—church, temple, mosque, the sacred space to transcend. "A temple is a landscape of the soul. When you walk into a cathedral, you move into a world of spiritual images. It is the mother womb of your spiritual life—mother church." Joseph Campbell recites in *The Power of Myth*.

Small red hands, outlines of women dot the walls. This is what home should feel like; the tour is nearly over.

~~~

The world is vast beneath the surface. Pech Merle, one of the only caves along France's Dordogne that remains open to the public, garners its name from the local Occitan language, *Pech* meaning *hill*, *Merle*, perhaps also meaning *hill* or *mound*. Before entering the mound-mound, we notice a seemingly unimportant oak tree—thin, well lodged in the rocky soil. Other slender oaks dot the plot of land. But it's too hot out to notice. We stop at the museum to pee and survey the map of red points along the river—a trail of caves now kept from our modern bodies.

We move through the giftshop into a surprisingly dark room with two glass walls. Shoppers watch us sit through the window. Warm and stuffy next to three Canadian families, a few from the states, and a large man from Australia. We make up the bevy of English speakers who will descend into the cave after the current French-speaking party emerges. The docent turns on a giant television as our eyes adjust to the radiation of blue light. She flashes through images, a pre-screening of what we will see "downstairs" to avoid extended viewing of the cave. Each exhale degrades cave paintings, our lifeforce ending theirs. Millenia ago, mouths full of fat and red ochre, we pressed our hands against the walls, exhaling red through bone straws to mark our place here. Breath to create and now degenerate: the womb, always a temporary space.

∿∿∿

We watch our step as cool air hugs us down the moist passage carved in rock. "The message of the caves is of a relationship of time to eternal powers that is somehow to be experienced in that place," Campbell reminds us, as the cavern expands and dims. We traverse the birth canal back to our origins the color of earth.

The woman in front of us is afraid of heights. The family behind us pushes closer in anticipation. Our skin cools from the July sun and relaxes to the voice of water dripping against subterranean silence. We continue soft, calculated steps entranced by the tour guide's flashlight— "Here we come into an enormous chamber, like a great cathedral, with all these painted animals."

An anthropology major on summer break moves light across the walls. Pointing out each shadowed figure "painted with the vitality of ink on silk in a Japanese painting—you know, just like that. A bull that will be twenty feet long, and painted so that its haunches will be represented by a swelling in the rock." Minerals engorge and engulf as the cavern continues. "You don't want to leave," Campbell says of his own journey into prehistory buried along the French countryside as the flashlight gleams against another rock.

The tour guide says at mark 13, "Next to us in red, you'll see a hand and thirteen dots. Below it we see women and bison." No one makes a sound. "Okay, please move along now." We don't want to leave, but she pushes along, her watch ticks to the rhythm of dripping water.

∿∿∿

The thrash of a cave bear's claw that fell off the edge of a rock millennia ago, a set of footprints so unbelievably small we think they must be that of a child, and what looks like an umbilical cord reaching from the sky.

The root of the oak tree.

Inside the mound there is a womb a tomb an umbilicus.

Breath the generate. Breath to disintegrate.

"The only light they had was a little flickering torch."

∿∿∿

*day earth was created*


      feathers dance
nothing into inchworms
whispering

        *sheeeeee shhhheee*           *shee*    *shaaa*   *shhhh*

    to people in their paper houses

              women
              circle    blow ochre    a puff
              across the face three red hawks

                    fly over
                    red red drops
                        dearer than life

*sexual birth*

pregnant     hormones
drawn to drink

our silly–faces' soul water
ignite        bawdy ecstatic
letters leaking                    seeping

(becoming)
                    ((((revealing))))

our meat
glinting gold on bathroom tile

       verbs weave

dissolve organ nouns            into odor  and pubic hair

slick and matted     salt and camphor

wind of labor
tongues
       red      wailing            watery  sex

           conjoining sentence

*Pleiades*

a story old as blood
seven sisters

turned stars—
the youngest

sewn of dust so
in love with a mortal she strays

dipping her jugs into the stream

again and again pouring one in water, one on land
for health
hope
opportunity
so naked her skin gleams one foot
in water, one on land
we see six        name seven—

before the moon
each inhale collecting bits of
the other six.

*The Alchemy of Dreams*

In a dream I force myself to pee through a catheter that moves up a wall like an IV line threaded in reverse; bearing down I feel a *pop*. My father cries behind me, "Congratulations! You just bled on your period panties." I pull off the thick black cotton briefs. Three spots of blood stare back at me.

In *Alchemy for Women*, Penelope Shuttle outlines a menstrual mandala to record dreams, menstruation, and corresponding symptoms in correlation with the phasing moon. Shuttle believes dreams ovulate and menstruate symbolically and attending to dreams eases the menstrual cycle. This also means everyone menstruates and ovulates in dreams, often in synchrony with the moon.

The dream passage between worlds bleeds just as we bleed through menstruation, miscarriage, and post-birth. By not attuning ourselves to blood, we project symbolic menstruation on the outer world: fracking, oil drilling, and war. By not attuning ourselves to blood, we bleed the world around us. I asked, what menstrual rags are we rejecting \ what garbage is menstrual / how are we ignoring our blood rites?

In a dream, I want to touch a prairie dog. I realize they're being trapped in cages in the yard. The cages are electrified. I cry "no no no no no no no," backing up the driveway.

An hour after waking, a red bath mat lay crumpled in the middle of my street.

*The blood skirt*
menstrual rag a red tag upon our honor
Falda Rojo is a talking horse beheaded
in *The Goose Girl*

*after losing her mother's menstrual rag in the river*
*a princess loses her identity*
*tends geese like a peasant*
*reclaims her voice in the womb of an iron stove.*

Each fairytale a fragment of cosmology.

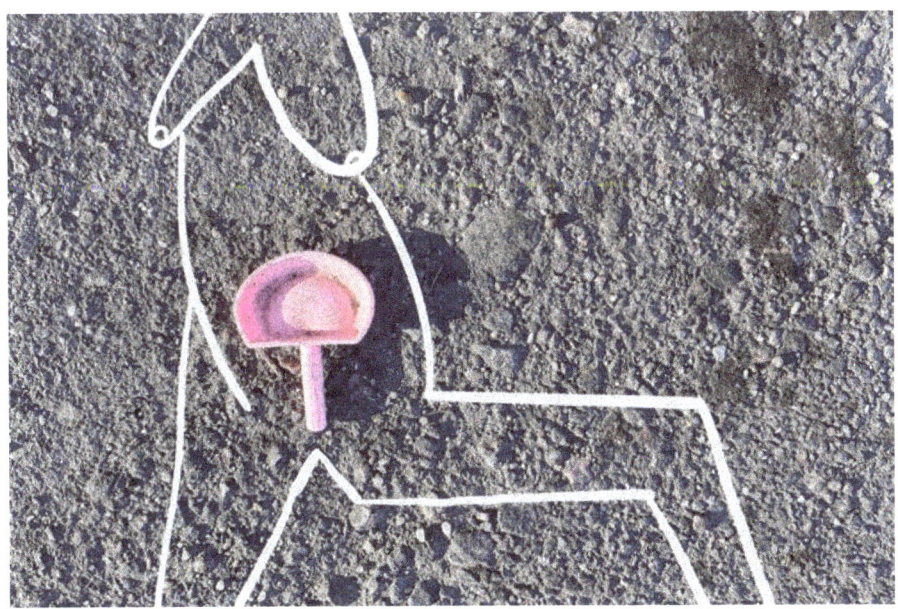

*skirt bleeds*

breast bleed     chest bleeds
eyes bleed     the image
of a woman outlined in charcoal
plump among flowers

1895 Georges Lacombe draws *First Thought for Isis*
liquid streaming
from her breast since
1943 there have been ten
sightings of Virgin Mother
figures bleeding
tears    hairlines     shedding     menstrual

layers

birthing     blood from stone
porcelain
gold leafed in
churches and cathedrals
a woman's hand extends
the world

*Embroidering the blood skirt*

cheap synthetic le Targét machine pleated
outlines of women's faces printed white on
black appear
upscale Parisian only fitting for a skirt
an American woman wears to France to see
*First Thought of Isis.*

Skirt becomes a ladder
lightning path
tree
which places masculine and
feminine
in opposition
left hip a woman
right hip man
the lightning path
a bean stock
tower
sacred way to
first creation
and back
again
Skirt holds
blood
masks—
they
say
all
early
petticoats
were
practical
red
later
royal.

*The origin of royal dress. West Africa: Dogon*
A woman stole a fibre skirt which was stained with the world's first menstrual flow. Putting it on herself and concealing her identity by this means, she reigned as queen and spread terror all around. But then men took the fibres from her, dressed themselves in the royal garment, and prohibited its use to women. All the men danced wearing the reddened fibres, and the women had to content themselves with admiring them. (Griaule 1965: 170)

—Chris Knight

*Rags:* scrap of cloth, early 14c., probably from Old Norse *rögg* «shaggy tuft,» slang for "tampon, sanitary napkin", 1930's "on the rag" 1948.


The tongue invents a wordless sensation.

> The tongue invents language. The tongue inverts the street glittered in menstrual rags.


"Menstruation has long been veiled by a mysterious silence in our culture. In fairy tales, myths, and folk tales this intimate female reality is concealed in symbols and metaphors."

*—The Mead of Poetry*


Ragging the menstrual rag
shame composes the counter.


In many traditions, female initiation is channeled through rituals
            I cannot bare
                        to throw away.

Some women soak plastic rags in water: pink juices feed flowers feed cats do a bit of skin changing.

The taste of menstrual blood is a spicy form of iron. Mouthfeel of birthing everything and nothing of me and not.


Four unopened pads: white squares line the green fence of the baseball field. Breadcrumbs of ovulation. On the other side of earth, girls beg for the gift of a sanitary napkin.

The *sanitary towel* was named in 1880, *sanitary* for *health* and *sane*.

>Insanity's shame
>metaphor's forgotten matter
>yards of red surveyor tape
>lick what would be
>mud if rain came *red*.

I photograph trash daily on the 3-mile circuit through my neighborhood, sometimes noting how garbage changes or doesn't. Sometimes I want to touch it, but never do. Somehow, I believe the earth is displaying/reclaiming these menstrual rags.

Thesmophoria, Θεσμοφορια, the ancient Greek menstrual rite left pigs for Demeter collected rotting flesh of piglets perhaps from days before or another season a sacrifice, organic trash, dinner for goddess nature.

Cherry paint circles squares cross hatching sidewalks in unintelligible language to the passerby—

Licorice strands. Decomposing silk roses fly from the cemetery up the hill trap themselves in fallen leaves until wind speaks again——*moovve——oooove  oooo*

>decomposing string
>Aranciada Rossa
>Blood Orange wrapper sings

I am a quarter orange sour candy crystalizing in the sun.

"You cannot deceive earth, you must respect earth, especially in spring when she is pregnant," Marija types on her Apple 2E.

Mr. Potato Head's missing ear is a womb's last thread to wisdom—which means *ear* in Sumerian, language of Inanna who put her ear to the ground before descending into menstrual death and resurrection.

Will our trash die to resurrection, or does its redness stand as reminder of aversion to the blood stains on pants, sheets, and dresses. Blood that stains our street in egotistical transgressions.

A shoe box falls apart among the prairie dog nation. A red river snake shimmering in grassless wonder
I wonder why no one picks up their trash.

I pause outside the bookstore. A man asks, "I've got to know, is it the reeeeead queen, or the RED queen," the owner bites her lip, "red" she says, sliding his receipt towards him.

There is a certain instinct in composition to pre-visualize the hieroglyphic cave painted woman popular in Paleolithic art, as well as carvings of the Neolithic period. How is this litter of me and not of me? I ask.

Focused always breasts, bellies, and vulvas because as Marija Gimbutas said, "The goddess was birth, death, regeneration."

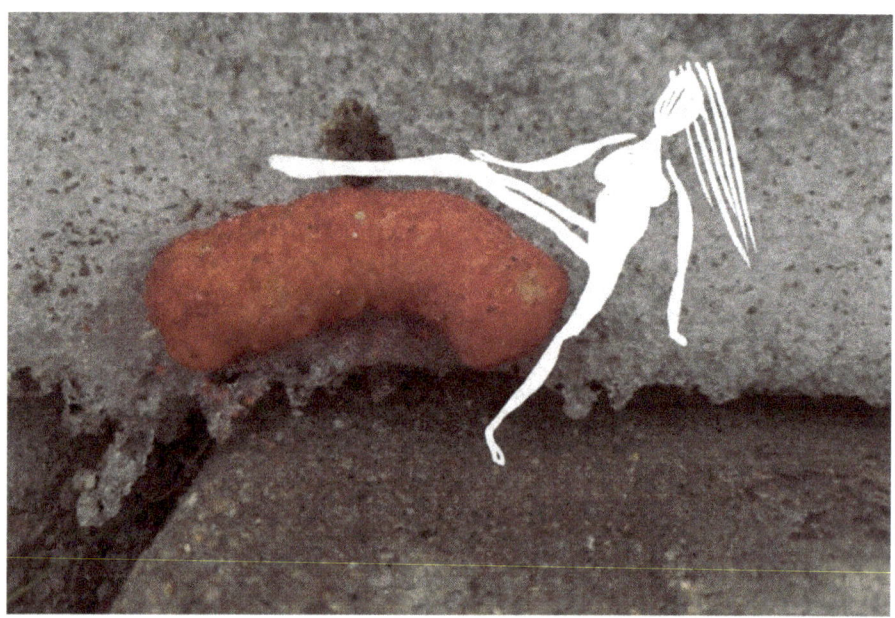

The garter is a rag, the ribbon a rag, why are auto-shop rags fundamentally red?

Plucked from the dance floor Edward usurped the garter from Elizabeth
"*Honi soit qui mal y pense!*"
Exclaimed a secret order, reversing gender Edward a queen, Elizabeth
England's great breasted king, *at her majesty's pleasure,* clouding notions of gender.

In the legend of the Green Knight and Sir Gawain, tested by lust and death,
the garter one temptation too many, Gawain bleeds from a nick on the neck.
"That's for the garter," the giant says.
*Shame be to him to thinks evil*     the menstrual rag!

The more I practice this ritual, the more I find I am honoring that which abhors me. I've never understood the carelessness of litter, and now give it a personal place of meaning as a gesture towards the collective attitudes of menstruation, birth, and the female form.

Everyone forgets the first alchemists in labs doing work, doing laundry, making gold from lead were women making clothes from rags making children from the belly of earth. Turning lead into gold of living.

The menarchal girl takes us back to first creation—time before time, tether to earth, she bleeds and we cut ourselves, join hands and travel to the sky together.

To let her go, we forget from where we came. This place of soil littered in wrappers.

Amidst the trash & rubble she screams: *The Paleolithic goddess was the creatrix.*

We mistake wind, rubber greasing asphalt, brush caught in spokes, the absence of silence:

"She's really asking us—is the way we're living the best way to live?"

¿que vida queremos?

When Spider Woman falls to earth, she must open her eyes to avoid psychosis: to red garbage filling streets, blood in sheets.

To silence the menarchal girl, rain comes black, white, toxic oil greed seeding silence.

The fate of Briar Rose is prophesized by a red crustacean emerging from the bath of an infertile queen.

Cursed by nature, the young girl turns a rusty key, pricks herself on the third Fate's spindle as the castle falls asleep. They dream an ovulatory splendor while impatient men die in the bramble trying to get in.

The menarche of first creation cannot be overthrown, no matter how overgrown the briar. In sleep small death, orgam of slumber until we wake to dream again—spinning.

Three red bottle caps and I'm supposed to flush my blood but instead it spills on the kitchen floor and I wonder if the land lady will notice the tinge of pink that remains when I am gone. And I wonder how many menstrual rags remain outside my window.

*Day 2*

I stare at the cotton pad on the counter. Blotched, red, pink, textured three pubic hairs compressed memoriam another pregnant friend's room painted blue poured over the pad on television mimics blood. Her child arrives in September. Red divines a spot of faith imaginary blue.

Syncopation strums the cervix, drum full to empty. The divination counts on belief outside a system outside a window a red tail talons the infant prairie dog. Eyes bulge the first sight of light. Sun shines red behind eyelids. In a dream, one day I may divine a child.

*Ovulatory Dream, Day 13*

The space between us is blue and green—

——malachite and chrysocolla——

A mineraloid joins semi-precious stone, a splash of finite biology.

Once color was not named—blue became lapis, red cardinal, yellow banana, green hope—the shade of ovulation.

"My green
is a leaf
resting
on your
fencepost,"
you say.

It is hot and leaves press between palms to a cool late summer's green which will hug the air after I leave you for a duckling in the parking lot. He grows a thirsty deep green. I cradle him.

Into a sinking feeling,

we drop.

Turtle eye lands green algae into robustness of a mosquito kissing my knee blue water, salted on skin.  Waking to forget—

before memory was erased, the feminine was the living presence of language.

> Green is an ovulatory color;
> the great prehistoric mother is being aroused.
> —Penelope Shuttle

*musgos*

pillows the shade of ovulation
remember me
dappling shale and shingle

lacking true roots
to rise and fall
like
ancient mothers
bled
into baskets of perfect
branches collecting
spongy green
enlivening gathering

remnants of seed

I slept in the basket
rising and falling to the vanishing
of a downy cocoon

water so green algae fluttered
between my legs
enlivening gathering me into
a breathing sea

I knew a dead caterpillar could never
butterfly, like moss torn from
shingles withers in sunlight.

While watching *Outlander* I wonder when Claire travels back in time if she researched the proper menstrual rags of 16th century Scottish Highlands or if she has to ask a maid. This leads me to a medieval forum in which scholars argue over several years between cotton and linen as viable, accessible, and affordable menstrual rags for women of the British Isle. I wonder if they used moss like the Indigenous women of America. One person notes, "They did rinse and reuse these cast-off scraps."

*Fox Woman Dreaming*


*I will be the woman of the house,* she said, red hair cascading her shoulders.
The man's head tilted towards this stranger

        her pelt on a nail behind the door.

The man blinked and realized she came from a place unfamiliar to him. She
called herself Fox Woman Dreaming and

                     handed him a skillet. His eyes softened
into the sweet aroma of her skin, hollyhock and raspberry. A
combination his nose had never known. As smoke rose from
the pan they talked laughed, cooked, and ate dinner. He felt
warm for the first time he could remember.


In time, her pelt began to smell. Fox Woman said nothing.

The couple was so happy, the man ignored the stench behind the door,
leaving it ajar long after sundown.

In the city a young woman thought, *I will be the woman of the house,*
boarding with two men who loved to dance all night with mead and
whiskey. They took her to party after party, some nights to the aquarium
where small fish swam in domes that made their faces so distorted, she would
get queasy and ask to go home.

Despite the man's newfound joy and laughter, he grew sick to his stomach as the pelt grew pungent. He worried the smell would never leave

his pillows, sheets, skin—the inescapable scent of fox filth. Even in the shower no amount of bathing could soap away her scent.

He complained and complained

like the young woman in the city who begged one night to leave the party. The men of the house ignored her until she bled through her jeans onto her new car seat, to which they replied, "we'll just buy another seat!" grinning.

She didn't know what to say as the man

complained so many times to Fox Woman, he woke

to the scent of nothing but the salt of his own arm.

Fox Woman Dreaming was gone, along with the memory of red, hollyhock and raspberry. He sniveled at the staleness he didn't remembered was the natural scent of air.

The young woman's housemates never bought her a new car seat. They continued to dance into the night. Brewing mead in the kitchen they laughed as she drove to the auto-shop and picked up two grey sheep skins, strapping one to her seat, one to the passenger's.

The man waited, staring at the nail behind the door. Remembering how deeply he loved Fox Woman Dreaming but worried she'd never been there at all. The nail began to rust.

The young woman in the city ran her hand through the sheepskin, pleased it looked like nothing ever happened. That night she drove towards the mountains and never returned.

As the air grew stale from Fox Woman's absence, the mead ran dry. The man waited by the door every night for a glimpse of the red hair woman and her pelt. The men in the city danced, as if nothing ever happened.

The young woman pressed the accelerator until
the wind caught her scent.

A hand knocked at her window. She saw the dark face of a woman bounding
alongside the car. She reached for the lock that was no longer there. The
window rolled down and the dark face of the woman with red cascading
hair reached her arm through the window, opening the door. The young
woman pressed the accelerator again wishing to wake from what seemed a
nightmare.

Fox Woman leapt into the car. The two were only ever seen in the Dreaming.

*aliento, day 12*

For thousands of years, we did not have what we call *language,* yet managed to communicate.

\*

A Brazilian girl in Crete draws diagrams of wind in crayon, believing wind speaks colored messages to the body. red. blue. yellow halos limbs.

She maps our island village; a treasure hunt singing cicadas beats me to dream of deafness el aliento de Sappho rising off the water, whispering to the orange and white kitten, fleas drinking his right eye.

In the sun I bare my belly to wind, waiting to float into an olive grove, tiers of ancestral farming once woman reigned.

As the sun falls into sea, I see the moon of *Midnight Poem,* which will not set for another two weeks. I do not sleep alone nor can I ever, the moon slowly inching its way from earth.

A diagram of ancient progress—wind and moon—outline of a battered shoe.

/Kaggen created the moon, stealing an eland bull's gallbladder.

Darkness eclipses sun. In another variant, his right shoe chafes and pinches, his heel bleeds—first Achilles.

Bird Daughter drops the shoe in a watering hole, enraging Watersnake who freezes the lake. The shoe retrieved is leathered icicle.

Wind Bird carries red icy shoe so high into night, it lights the world in a crescent.

It melts, dies, people cry and Watersnake turns it into a fountain. Now moon cycles until the end of time.

The moon, same moon everywhere/in every land; at home hawks perch on lampposts, trees bloom sprigs of white plastic thrashing harsh/high desert air.

A knit cap, weathered blue sprouts.

Time too grows on the moon; wind tires of our assonance.

*the machine embroiders*

*whuuuuuuuuuuuo whuuuuuuuuuuuuo whuuuuuuuuuuuo whuuuuuuuuuuuo*
on red mesh
sweet potato bags

tubers
sustenance of women, collected
world-wide dug discovered
piled into dilly bags carried
back to camp roasted fried
consumed in one night
to dig again tomorrow
from a red mesh bag
or soil.

       The machine embroiders from digital memory in pink thread
       trinity of black white red. Language is digital—on off yes no 1 0 01
       coded.

       The hand weaves threads through mesh creating a solid form
       holding plastic matter
       holy undecomposable
       trash.

       The embroidery sits in the hoop for a very long time
       on the floor
       waiting to become a dilly bag
       waiting for a woman to care
       to find the words to say

       *whuuuuuuuuuuuo whuuuuuuuuuuuo whuuuuuuuuuuuo*
       *whuuuuuuuuuuuo*
       on red mesh.

*Prayer for Menstruation*


Half moon
early light

speckles
egg
from night

builds a belly
iron rust coils mud
water silt
slides
into the kiln

engorges breasts
spurts fire wet
and sanguine
scored in slip
quenching
cools rests on
mesa's edge

all that almost was
until it comes anon.


So the moon bears the picture of Water-Woman ...
The "face of the Moon" bears the mark of the first menstruation of the woman..

—George Dorsey

The drum is a model is a ball is a womb—a hollow. The bow stretches embers, inflection inhales.

La lengua divesadero es el binaro.

The pulse is an absence of light exhaling. A clot mirrors, constellates on skin.

A star is a fragment          re—fle—jado,

empathy for wind.

*Day Sixteen*

In the origin of separation language recovers.
*Teeeeeeeeeeeewaaaaaaaaaaaaaah*                    *shoooo*

Wire wraps the bark burnt red in summer. Trees' eyes illuminate dandelion
lashes, clumped grasses germinate through seed casing. The squirrel with one
ear flicks his tail to the metronome.  The morgue that touched on impossible
things in our pelvis. The ovum, pocks like the moon face, pruning in wait
for disseminate culture.

*Separation* is elemental, splitting off as a method of differentiating from the
mass, and using taboos to regulate boundaries of behavior and establish
categories. The natural phenomenon of entrainment of the inner menstrual
cycle with the outer lunar cycle is a gift of nature that allowed ancestral females
to comprehend patterns of synchrony, beginning with the idea that all blood
is menstrual blood.

—Judy Grahn

The moon is the first being to die, and the first be reborn.
—Mircea Eliade

A brush. A rise.  A confluence of bodies. The merge is stronger with the consolidation of hydrogen in the blood. The markers are a drum, a radiation, a rhythm, syncopation's end. All must separate to begin.

*day three, first snow*

la primera
                bone
        caught       blanca   black cold
cenizas sueños                    smoke steams sangre
        first snow  clumps me                        in la copita

coag•u•late


        san • guin • ario

under blankets           blanca still, silent she's *sssssssss sssssssss sssssss*
  las almentas mas
                smell of •
her body
lim • pieza
cold

sucios nunca.

I dream my mother and I are forensic scientists. There's been a murder in the home of a neighbor who used to pick me up after school. She fed me graham crackers and Gatorade while I binged old shows on Nickelodeon. A dirty red rug covers the sliding glass door. Someone has told us a bit about the murder as we cross the cement stones from our yard to theirs; I forget everything as we enter. A group of women sit in a circle on benches, like in a sauna at the club I went to once in the Berkeley Hills. Three dead women are strewn across a wooden platform. All wear shades of red in shiny lycra suits, like the backup dancers in the JLo and Shakira half-time show so many people criticized for oversexualizing the female body on national television (though they seemed to enjoy Janet Jackson's nipple slip). I lock eyes with the women. Their pony tails slicked back with strong-hold gel. I realize I am next.

If we do not know what it is to bring forth the unknown from our own bodies, can't be comfortable with this process we will just continue to perpetuate the old ways and we'll all be in trouble. Because while it's scary for us women it's far scarier for men who have never had the experience of giving birth and who must be very frightened.

—*The Feminine Face of God*

*In time*

making the animal passage in hands
taste of blue      resurfaces
bells on ankles engorge
appetite of weather

men dance women's seclusion

mother root harnesses
          lengua          agua fría de aves

we drink into new—ancient order—

blood
                    water
                                        breast

          familiarity of    breath


rain dances rivers        the menstrual flow of earth.


The first (and second and third) appearance of a girl's menstrual blood is interpreted as 'an opening to First Creation'; she now exists inside First Creation, constantly changing her form, and this fills her with strong *n/om* (lifeforce among the Ju/'hoan Bushmen).

—Camilla Power

*Day Eleven*

The hair is a cycle is a ring round the pubis round the crown. A memory transference of a population: carbon nitrogen allopathic oxygen hydrogen the smell of rotting eggs. Death occurs on the scalp in the ring there is a shadow silky taste of winter. The dermal papilla seeds a single hair birthed to death. The scalp circulates ends, without nutrients we do not bleed feed one cell, *red.*

You should feel all of your body exactly as it is, and pay attention.
—Yurok Woman, *Blood Magic*

*Day Four*

Inflammation is a storm is a letter guarded by a letter startled by sound.

*HEEEEEEEEEEEEEEEWAH*
                    *SOOOOOOOOOOOOOOOOOOOOM*

The loss is umber dried and matted on the lining of the cotton of the body of the belly of the brood.

*ochre*

                      congeals

brush tip

       with spit

       springs

       rivers pages

              into song


          luna's incandescence glitters

         mica in the white of eyes


the sclera rings pupils

eclipses


through pinhole

cameras


mother blinks

        the sun red and still.


In some societies the royal or aristocratic --- that is to say, the collective --- menstruant personified the central cosmological principles. The queen, the holy mother, and the priestess were the living emissaries of deity, and deity likewise communicated through the externalized embodiment of the collective menstruant. The king and the priest, pharaoh, or holy men were also living emissaries of deity. In many areas, members of menstrual elites were considered divine. Like the earlier menstruant, they could cause and prevent flood, famine, disease, and the movements of planets and seasons.

                                       —Judy Grahn

*medicina de los sueños*

the cure for anything: salt in water

la cura: cosa sal en agua

cure for sleeping with white sage, nest burial stream of contemplation

los sueños complimentado

cure for bleeding: blood

cura

sangrado        sangre.

*depression in dreams bleeds*

ligaments sap for days
as bark peels and cinders

sadness fills
robin eggs blue

a cup of blood circles roots
a woman's weight swarms
the tree until it bleeds
open the mouth of earth

*how I wish you were a man—*

she sings

the biplane wings
coax clouds into formation

wide eyes hunched, hawks circle
another prairie dog found dead.

*day twenty-nine and 1/2*

I stare at a list of questions for a very long time until we start coming
into our nature: house of the generated soul.

The language of nature that makes us known to
la lengua         the primordial tongue
of dirt—

temenos severed; wired off from the forest
becoming dust                                        no longer
soil

our particles digress into

sundried fragments

letter *s sssss*     in pavement *sss   s           s            su          scu*

*scccuuuuuuu uuuuuuuu*

One view, then, is that human culture, including menstrual synchrony, was
invented and shaped by men. The other —which is argued here— culture is
based primarily on solidarity, that this solidarity is in the first instance sexual
(manifesting itself among women as menstrual synchrony), that women's
ability to go 'on strike' is the primordial guarantee of their sexual solidarity
and that the necessary periodic 'sex strike' initially took the form of collective
and synchronized menstrual withdrawal.

—Chris Knight

*An ear dreaming*

*heeeeeeeeewaaaaaaaaaaaaah shooooooo*

thin drops engorge blue light
bitter streams kissing
skin
negating gravity

bioluminescent
spirits dipping
into
horizontal love.

The me bleeding with you can forest days of air hunger.

*sheeeeeeeeeewaaaaaaaaaaa louuuuuuuu*

*on lamenting silence*

We tie a red string from one pinkie to the other
beat our fingers closer
then further
apart
*la lengua de las mariposas*
licks our strings.

Syncopating we
blur      our nature bends,  cleaves
into this quiet exercise of patience.

*Sadness is a lust for language* she says
each vein the color of *please*
we beat our wings tied
from  blood  and  belly  string

innate animates; a loop being forms–
feeding, refeeding our cycle of one
hand—heart—string—hand—heart
all at once, self-sustenance.

  She dances a rhythmic tension,
  shapes begin in clouds,
  snaking emptiness into sound weather
  a rhythm circles
  hand—heart—string—hand—heart
  words rattle from wings
  language gapes between fibers.

The monarch butterfly creates a collective womb that is invisible: the creative
capacity of collective birthing.

—James O'Hern

73

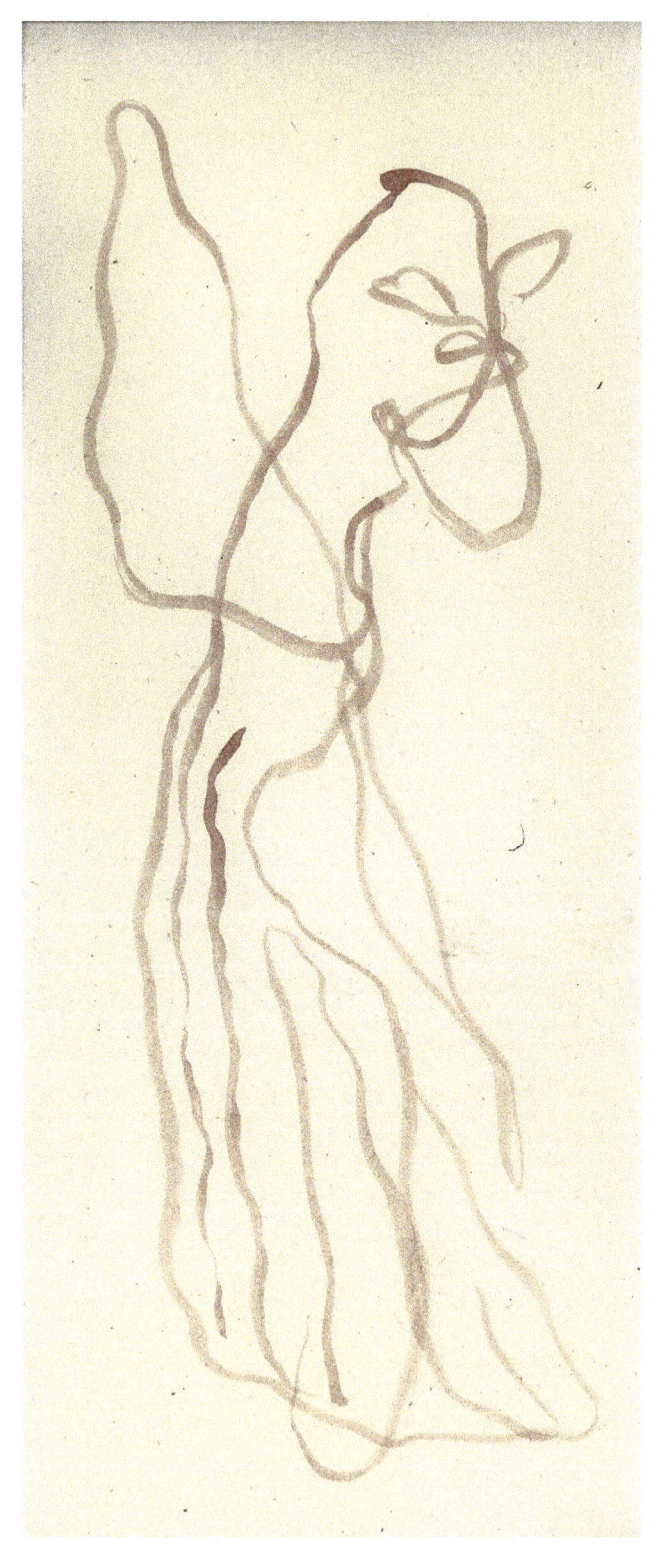

74

*day 15*

pinch     gnawing
          springs

eternity's hand kneads my insides raw—

*thrum thrum thrum drum smack bawlk crack rum rum rum rum ruuuuuuuuuuuuum room*

                              *drop* wait

                              if it would bleed today
                              I should rain.

The belly round, light and fluid. Charcoal lines torso. A stroke. A smear. A mistake in order as body pools between folds. Skin sheltered. Fear of man. Draws down circles, red. Three spots on the floor boards, turning heads. Three turkey vultures overhead. The window is a frame is a border is a hole longing to understand the pain he must feel unable to bleed.

*lonely day fullness*

chest     specks      fluids  between           collar bone and breast
    a white marble crucifix, degrades in vinegar—a man says I'll never understand
*Piss Christ* like Sister Wendy did—

      never know decreation, dismantling cells

a reformation      contemplation of what it is to be born       the cunt

a blush rock      touchstone     an ancestor's hold

        the robin's red breast

a ruin   of imagination      cryptic delicacy of her weathered claws cringe

*I will return to dust soon, just like you!*    I sing   to the pretty   dead    bird

flatted in the driveway

     *you will learn to understand the sound of quarters* her limp beak squeaks

.

      a drop of water  *gorge   ourge  engorge ogre    forge orge    orge*
  *orange*

        the moon winks the sun to slumber quarter
     past new

*day eight*
*unexpected continuation of sound*


escaping the hole of abyss
it seems a whole day has gone by

not yet
behind the skin
a shawl
the a(r)mo(u)r of flight—

women leave their sacred
forest
      take over camp
play and
ritual
dance
one becomes another
      wax and feather skin
      in *she* there is an animal

you cannot kill.

*mating season*

late winter. a peep in snowfall. a gadfly or frenzy;
*estrus* lasts a single hour
three thousand          six       hundred seconds to repopulate
the prairie dog nation

hope          la lengua maternal

bark          cry               belch                    chatter


a prayer: only one-half-litter lives to summer

*confusing our blood with blood*

in the dream        a man punctures my uterus
a knife through the door   I wake      fall back cramping.

*Jesús murió por nuestros pecados,* which always sounded like *pescados*
      filleting ourselves     in original sin
          balance of red          unending
     la crucifixión erased our need to bleed
        and yet she asks the sea of *red* continue—

so we bleed in streets         borders neighbors
      gnawing our meat to return her water to soil
       we must be
               lost translations.

A lark. A starling. A squirrel on the bed. A tendency to curl into words, hearing is a form of feeling. A spark. A spatter. A spree of imagination.

*day 22*

       I clamor for *red*
falling into amazement
grasping my hands
which are her hands
which are your hands
las manos de sueños son *la man(n)a* of my grand
mother tongues
la lengua de aves es la lengua
of gold

                 water is gold
                     the blood of the earth
                         hearing us.
                           —Cecilia Vicuña

*ambas y nada*

larynx mirrors      | cervix mirrors

a cave      a speck of sesame
a bead                |      plucked from blushing
sunflower
cracked between lip and lip
teeth and teeth
sucked
into the belly, like Lone Star Swan, tagged
painted over | a scream rattles
the throat the cunt
venus thistle
red blooming
slow.

*Rites of Passage*

young male prairie dog
em          barks   cries   burrows
himself into

suburbia
digs
caverns making
boys into men


a loneliness of species
bleeds
to the invisible creator

boys
scrounge new
order
to become

to initiate
gifts
women bore


do you remember the sound of the red wing?

*shee shee shh sh shhhhhh*


Female prairie dogs exhibit philopatry, defined as fidelity
to one area, and do not commonly disperse from their
birth territories. When or before they become sexually
mature, male prairie dogs disperse away from their birth
ward, thus avoiding any chance of inbreeding. Female
prairie dogs will generally remain in their birth area for
their entire lives, living with their mothers, sisters, aunts,
cousins, and nieces. This localization strategy is called
matrilocal (*matri-* from Latin for *mother*), and most
female prairie dogs are matrilocal for their entire lives.

—John Hoogland

*day 34*

grey cat in the grass
floats on pink light
heron's moon
      strings across water
wheat downtrodden dries
every border a scar
slow         sponging
circle

Yahweh's mother sister        daughter


on the hut of pelican thunder
her insides gold behind the mountainside
egg         shell      lining
body

of such        coherent
consistent          manners

rupture milk


The legend was that in time of famine, the mother pelican wounded herself, striking her breast with the beak to feed her young with her blood to prevent starvation. Another version of the legend was that the mother fed her dying young with her blood to revive them from death, but in turn lost her own life.

— William Saunders

In anger she retaliates, striking her young dead, but after three days regrets her actions and pierces her own side with her beak. As she allows her blood to drip on the young, they revive and she dies, having made the ultimate sacrifice for her children.

—*The Book of Beasts*

*cuerpo*

sacrament of Adam
red   drawn tree      a drop
dews

a lynx round the belly of the moon

but what of Lilith?
the birds seed
devil fingers
red tails pecking
prey

at birth
blood floods Christmas
red paper crumples
streets wash us
snow blankets
clean

the sun
slinks open caverns

a second talon clutches
home

a sugared egg
cracks, illuminates

if the moon were hollow she'd
make a mouth for you.

*day 27*


*The moon is the brain*
between amygdala and pituitary
purple and soft
back of a cattail in winter


mother's body
dissolves        particulate
low land waters
like octopus tentacles
sway into pods of kelp
she dies to her children—

every vessel
a cosmology
birth


In her body woman carries the secret knowledge of fertility and growing. Woman is like the field. The field and the woman both carry the seed. The seed is at home in her body and in the earth's body. The seed feeds off the moist nurturing food her blood carries and the earth carries. Her body naturally harbors the seed in her womb. The seed grows. The mystery astounds her. And she is the mystery. Wisely, the fields belong to woman.

—Betty De Shong Meador

*Waiting*

to come home

here      is not where
we left it
            nor where
we
            are

the lady sees spots

                        that are not there

                        tal vez los secretos

                        born from lips in
                        need of sequester

                        quizás las hermanas
                        said
                        our blood profane
                        kept sacred secrets

                        twisting words in
                        translation

                        las hermanas

know what was

            will be

            waiting.

We need all the tools of humankind: arrow *and* loom, hierarchy *and* consensus, competition *and* cooperation, tenderness *and* ferocity, leisure *and* discipline. Men and women are not in deadly opposition. They are dancing the steps that give us human culture, that allow us to abstract «concepts» from our metaforms -- nonsexual unions of the gender-minds.

—Judy Grahn

*remembrance for a loss of sound*

                                        *heeeeeeeeeeeee waaaaaaaaah*

*shooooooooom*


a prayer for the dying coyote:

on the horizontal discourse of la lengua rudia

a binary prevails        the *tapua*———a crux, a curse a silent correspondence
of difference between

letters———Womankind's abandonment :

                        this mound letting     seizing our tongues'

                        secrets wound her

                        empty                  alone




                                        silence bleeds away

                        synchrony of power.

Polynesian tapua, means both "sacred" and "menstruation," in the sense, as some traditions say, of "the woman's friend."
Besides sacred, taboo also means forbidden, valuable, wonderful, magic, terrible, frightening, and immutable law.

> Taboo is the emphatic use of imperatives, yes or no, you must or you must not.

> Taboo draws attention, strong attention, and is in and of itself a language for ideas and customs.
>
> —Judy Grahn

> Paradox alone can achieve unity.
>
> —Keith Critchlow

*sheeeeeeeeee waaaaaaaaaah shoooooooooom*

hand      hand      heart         string      hand      heart

hand          heart      string        hand      heart
hand          heart          string      hand
    heart
      hand   heart        string      hand   heart
      heart      string         hand   heart

*heeeeeee waaaaaaaaaa shooooooooooooom*

to remember wind      recovers sound

      to recover sound

      nuestra lengua bleeds

When language recovers, the body makes sense.

# PEOPLE OF NOTE

**Chris Knight** is a social anthropologist whose thesis advisor asked him not to write about menstruation in his analysis of Lévi-Strauss' *Mythologiques*. He did anyway, and wrote *Blood Relations*, a controversial account of the human revolution centered on menstruation, cyclicity, and the moon.

**Camilla Power** is a social anthropologist who loves rabbits and the moon. Her work focuses on the Female Cosmetic Coalition and the sex strike model developed by Knight. Together they run Radical Anthropology Group out of London.

**Ian Watts** is presumably the world's ochre expert. After reading and early draft of *Blood Relations* he told Chris the dates were all wrong, the revolution did not begin in Europe, but in Africa centuries earlier. Through his study of ochre in Africa he proved both Chris' theories and his own doubts—the revolution indeed happened in Africa a very long time ago.

**Marija Gimbutas** was a Lithuanian archeologist and anthropologist who unearthed hundreds of goddess figurines across Europe, developing the theories of matrilineal society existing in the Neolithic period among Europe in which the goddess was worshiped and societies did not bother with war. From the figurines she decoded a symbolic language and was largely discredited by her peers while also securing tenure at UCLA until the end of her life.

**Judy Grahn** wrote the book most associated with menstruation, *Blood Bread and Roses.*

**Cecilia Vicuña** is a poet and artist from Chile known for her work with giant swaths of unspun red wool as well as installations of the Andean knotting of the Quipu.

**James O'hern** is Vicuñas partner and a poet.

**Penelope Shuttle** is a British poet who works in the realm of dreams and menstruation and often wrote with her late husband, poet **Peter Redgrove**.

**Keith Critchlow** was an architect and scholar of sacred geometry.

**Martin Shaw** is a mythologist and wilderness rites of passage guide who once lived four years in a tent to better understand his place in nature. He says the crone is the first character everyone meets when entering the forest.

# Reading List

*About to Happen,* Cecilia Vicuña
*Alchemy for Women: Personal Transformation Through Dreams and the Female Cycle,* Shuttle & Redgrove
*Basic Color Terms: Their Universality and Evolution,* Berlin and Kay
*Blood Bread and Rose,* Judy Grahn
*Blood Magic,* Gottlieb & Buckley
*Blood Relations,* Chris Knight

*Courting the Wild Twin,* Martin Shaw

*Here all Dwell Free,* Gertrude Muller Nelson
*Human Origins,* Power, Finnegan, & Callan
*Inanna and Ecology of the Erotic,* Judy Grahn
*Language of the Goddess,* Marija Gimbutas
*Myths & Texts,* Gary Snyder

*The Read Thread,* Cecilia Vicuña
*The Wise Wound,* Shuttle & Redgrove
*Thesmophoria,* Betty de Shong Meador
*Time too Grows on the Moon,* Ian Watts

*On Lamenting Silence* first appeared in issue #32 of *Q/A poetry journal*.
*Gadflies,* first appeared as one poem in *UndercoverWex* a women's mag in Wexford Ireland.
*Gadflies, Pecados,* first appeared in the *Aunt Flo Anthology* under different titles.
*In Time* was first published in *Alchemy Spoon* Issue 3.
*Depressions in Dreams Bleed, Mating Season,* and *Rites of Passage* were first published in *Burrow Magazine* as "The Prairie Dog Poems"
*Hvísla* and an early version of *medecina de los sueños* titled *night spell* first appeared in *Oracle Magazine*.
*Mound Mound* was first published in *Cauldron Anthology*.
*Day 22* was first published in *Ligeia Magazine*.
Visual poems from this book were first published in *Pomeleon Journal*.
*sucio* was first published in and issue by *apo press.

# ACKNOWLEDGEMENTS

Thank you to Chris, Camilla, and the folks at RAG for their continued help and study of menstruation & human origins. Thank you to my JKS family: Andrew for overseeing my critical exploration of the Wawilak Sisters in Vicuña's work during my MFA thesis, and J'Lyn for closely reading these pages as my thesis advisor alongside our prairie dog stories, and continued friendship. Anne for candid talks on menstruation and poetry. Gratitude to Emily for navigating our critical thesis papers together and Ada for reading early versions of this manuscript. Michelle, for inspiring *on lamenting silence* and allowing me to share this work with your undergraduate students. Lisa, thank you for helping me push the formal sonnet which digressed into the poem *on lamenting silence* has become.

Thanks to Mom, Bayje & Chris for the tour of Pech Merle, and the crew at Mudhouse Residency '19 for listening to the earliest versions of the *mound mound* essay and inspiring *aliento, day 12.*

Gratitude to Trese & the twins for giving me a home in the red house nestled between prairie dogs and hawks while I wrote this book (and thinking the anthropology of menstruation is cool).

To the dedicated folks at FlowerSong: thank you for believing in a little book about language and menstruation, the borders between languages and bodies. Edward–thank you for your tireless work to bring books into the world and catching every last typo! And thank you Priscilla for a thoughtful and poetic book design.

Thank you, Cecilia, for your continued work and support in the realm of menstruation, and Lyla for always answering my emails.

And endless gratitude to Jacob, without whom this book would be nothing more than an ovulatory dream.

# ABOUT THE AUTHOR

Amy Bobeda holds an MFA from the Jack Kerouac School of Disembodied Poetics at Naropa University where she directs the Naropa Writing Center and sometimes teaches process-based art, writing, & pedagogy. Her work has been featured in TYPO, Entropy, Full-Stop, Columbia Review, and elsewhere. She's also the author & artist of forthcoming books from Spuyten Duyvil, Ethel Press, & Finishing Line Press. She's the founder of Wisdom Body Collective with a group of radical women writers & artists who create and midwife somatic, contemplative, process-based work. Raised on the Amah Mutsun land of the Pajaro Valley, she can most often be found walking, running, & exploring through the cross sections between languages, art, eco-poetics, & menstruation in land-locked places.

www.ingramcontent.com/pod-product-compliance
Lightning Source LLC
Chambersburg PA
CBHW051635120626
46551CB00014B/2094